anythink

D0116871

MOOSE

by Josh Gregory

Children's Press®

An Imprint of Scholastic Inc.

Content Consultant
Dr. Stephen S. Ditchkoff
Professor of Wildlife Sciences
Auburn University
Auburn, Alabama

Photographs ©: cover: National Geographic Creative; 1: Michal_K/
Shutterstock, Inc.; 2, 3 background: Elena Panphilova/Dreamstime;
4, 5 background: DP RM/Alamy Images; 6, 7: blickwinkel/Alamy
Images; 8, 9: Terry A Parker/age fotostock; 10, 11: George Sanker/
Minden Pictures; 12: Yva Momatiuk & John Eastcott/Minden Pictures;
14, 15: Kevin Maskell/Alamy Images; 16: Jeff Vanuga; 18, 19: Jim
Brandenburg/Minden Pictures/National Geographic Creative; 20,
21: Patrick Endres/age fotostock; 23, 24, 25, 26, 27: DP RM/Alamy
Images; 28: George Sanker/Nature Picture Library; 31: Jeff Vanuga;
32: Charles Melton/Alamy Images; 34, 35: FLPA/Mark Newman/
age fotostock; 36, 37: Alaska Stock Images/National Geographic
Creative; 38, 39: DP RM/Alamy Images; 40, 41: Sumio Harada/
Minden Pictures; 44 background, 45 background: Elena Panphilova/
Dreamstime; 46: Michal_K/Shutterstock, Inc.

Library of Congress Cataloging-in-Publication Data
Gregory, Josh, author.
  Moose / by Josh Gregory.
    pages cm. — (Nature's children)
  Summary: "This book details the life and habits of moose"—
Provided by publisher.
  Includes bibliographical references and index.
  ISBN 978-0-531-21393-3 (library binding : alk. paper) —
ISBN 978-0-531-21496-1 (pbk. : alk. paper)
1. Moose—Juvenile literature. I. Title. II. Series: Nature's children
(New York, N.Y.)
  QL737.U55G75 2016
  599.65'7—dc23
                                    2014044035

All rights reserved. Published in 2016 by Children's Press, an imprint
of Scholastic Inc.

Printed in China 62
SCHOLASTIC, CHILDREN'S PRESS, and associated logos are
trademarks and/or registered trademarks of Scholastic Inc.

1 2 3 4 5 6 7 8 9 10 R 25 24 23 22 21 20 19 18 17 16

Moose

Class	Mammalia
Order	Artiodactyla
Family	Cervidae
Genus	Alces
Species	Alces alces
World distribution	Parts of North America, Asia, and Europe
Habitat	Forests
Distinctive physical characteristics	Heavy body weighing up to 1,300 pounds (590 kilograms); humped shoulders; large head with long face and drooping muzzle; wide, flat antlers; dark brown or grayish-brown fur, with rare examples of all-white or all-black fur; sharp hooves; relatively short tail; long ears; loose flap of skin called a bell hanging from neck
Habits	Male uses antlers to fight off enemies and show dominance over rivals; usually solitary during most of the year; most active at sunrise and sunset; spends most of its time eating or searching for food; communicates by making noises or leaving scent trails
Diet	Herbivorous; mostly eats stems, twigs, leaves, and other parts of trees and bushes; sometimes eats aquatic plants in habitats where they are common

Contents

CHAPTER 1

Clash in the Forest

It is a crisp fall day in the middle of October. A cool breeze rustles the changing leaves as the sun begins to set on the forests of the Rocky Mountains, near the border between the United States and Canada. In a clearing, two huge bull moose stand face-to-face. The moose paw at the ground with their sharp hooves and let out low, grunting sounds as they stare each other down. Suddenly, they both point their heads downward and run directly at each other. A loud crack can be heard as the moose's antlers crash together. The moose twist and turn their heads, then pull back and ram together again. Eventually, one of the moose catches its rival off guard and jabs its shoulder with a pointy antler tip. The wounded moose cannot continue the fight. It walks away to rest and heal as the victor approaches a nearby female.

Bull moose must use all of their strength to defeat rivals.

Dwarfing Other Deer

Moose are the deer **family**'s largest **species**. These enormous animals can weigh as much as 1,300 pounds (590 kilograms). Males are usually heavier than females. On average, a moose is about 8 to 10 feet (2.4 to 3 meters) long, and it stands about 7 feet (2 m) tall at the shoulder.

Adult moose usually have dark fur, ranging from grayish brown to almost black. They have slightly lighter coloring on their legs and **muzzle**. On rare occasions, a moose might be covered in white fur. All moose have large heads with long faces. Most also have a loose flap of skin called a bell that hangs down from their neck.

Like other deer species, male moose grow bony structures called antlers from the top of their head. A moose's antlers are larger than those of any other animal. They are mostly wide and flat, with pointed tips.

Adult male
6 ft. (1.8 m)

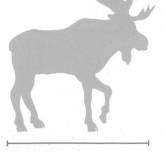
Male moose
7 ft. (2 m) tall at shoulder

10 ft. (3 m) long

A moose's bell and wide, flat antlers set it apart from other deer.

From Europe to America

Moose live in cold **habitats** where there are plenty of plants for them to eat. This means they are common in forests throughout the chilly northern parts of the world. The perfect moose habitat is home to a variety of trees and bushes. It is also located near a body of water such as a lake or a river. Some moose also live in swamps or high in mountains.

Moose are mainly found in the northern regions of North America and Europe, as well as some parts of northern Asia. In North America, they are common in Alaska and Canada. They can also be found in the forests in and around the Rocky Mountains in the western United States. In Europe, they are found in Scandinavia and several surrounding countries. Moose are also commonly found in Russia and Ukraine.

Snow is a common sight in most habitats where moose are found.

CHAPTER 2

The Mighty Moose

Though they are large, powerful animals, moose are not dangerous hunters. Instead, they are **herbivores**. They search out and eat hundreds of different kinds of plants. The exact food they eat depends on where they live. It also depends on the time of year. For example, moose might survive harsh winters by eating twigs. These are still in good supply even after the weather gets cold and snow starts to fall. In warmer times, when green plants are easy to find, moose eat more leaves. They also eat a variety of aquatic plants during the summer.

Sometimes moose don't get all of the nutrients they need by eating plants. In these cases, they visit mineral licks. Mineral licks are areas of soil that are rich in minerals such as salt. Animals eat the soil to get the nutrients they need.

Moose like to feed on the plants that grow in ponds and lakes.

Perfect Plant Eaters

Because moose are so large, they need to eat a lot of food to stay nourished. A fully grown moose might eat around 44 pounds (20 kg) of food every day! This means that a moose cannot survive by simply nibbling on a few leaves here and there. Luckily, the animal has many traits that help it consume large amounts of tasty plants. For example, a moose's upper lip is **prehensile**. It can grab onto plants and pull them into the mouth. A moose does not have upper teeth in the front of its mouth. Instead, it has a hard, bony plate. The moose presses its bottom front teeth against the plate to tear off a bite of food. It then uses the flat teeth at the back of its mouth to chew its food before swallowing. Because a moose eats hard, pointy plant parts such as twigs, it also has a tough tongue and lips to protect its mouth from damage.

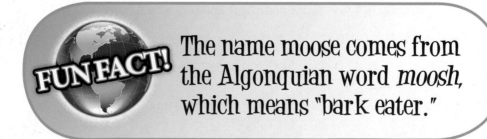

FUN FACT! The name moose comes from the Algonquian word *moosh*, which means "bark eater."

A moose can twist and turn its lips in several directions.

Observing Their Environment

Like all animals, moose rely on a number of senses to help them navigate, search out food, and avoid danger. Smell is one of a moose's strongest senses. The nostrils at the end of its muzzle are very large. This means there is plenty of room for air to meet the **cells** in the moose's nose that detect scents.

Moose also have extremely good hearing. Their long ears have a curved shape that helps capture sounds. Moose can rotate their ears to hear sounds coming from all around them. As a result, they can easily tell which direction a sound is coming from. This helps them watch out for **predators** that might be trying to sneak up from behind or from the side.

Moose do not have very good eyesight. However, because a moose's eyes are set on either side of its head, it can see to the left and the right at the same time.

A bull moose sniffs the air for the scent of nearby females.

Moose in Motion

Because of their weight and bulky shape, it might seem natural to assume that moose are slow movers. This is not the case at all. Moose are actually fast, nimble runners. They can sprint at speeds of up to 35 miles (56 kilometers) per hour for short distances. They can also jog at around 20 miles (32 km) per hour for longer distances. Moose can be relatively quiet when they move, especially in areas with little vegetation. However, they make more noise while crashing through dense forests at top speed.

In addition to their impressive movement on land, moose are very good at swimming. They are able to swim for long distances without stopping. They can also dive underwater and hold their breath for more than half a minute at a time. These skills help moose feed on underwater plants.

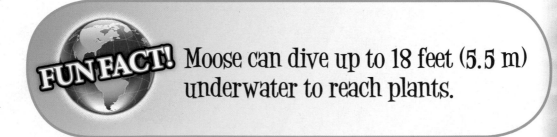

FUN FACT! Moose can dive up to 18 feet (5.5 m) underwater to reach plants.

Moose can swim across wide lakes to reach their destinations.

Formidable Fighters

The forest can be a dangerous place, even for big, strong animals like moose. A number of fearsome predators see moose as a tasty meal. Moose must keep an eye out for black bears, grizzly bears, and wolves. In some parts of the world, they also face off against cougars and tigers.

Moose are far from easy targets for these predators. When they have room to move, they can try to run away from threats. But when they need to, moose are more than capable of holding their own against even the deadliest foe. A moose's sharp hooves and pointy antlers provide natural weapons in a fight. When surrounded, the moose can kick backward or forward with its legs. It can also push or stab with its antlers. These powerful strikes can seriously wound or even kill enemies.

A female moose defends itself against an attack from a gray wolf pack.

Surviving the Elements

Living mainly in cold habitats, moose often face harsh, freezing weather during winter. Luckily, they are well equipped to deal with the challenges of a cold, snowy home. To protect against the cold, they have plenty of thick, heavy fur. This keeps heat from escaping their bodies and prevents their skin from getting wet.

A moose's legs are very helpful during winter. Sometimes there are several feet of snow on the ground. As a moose walks, its feet sink into it. Luckily, the animal's legs are incredibly long—long enough to keep the rest of the moose up and out of the snow.

Despite being useful weapons for defense, male moose shed their heavy antlers every winter. They do not grow new ones until spring. Growing antlers takes a huge amount of energy and can only occur once nutrient-rich green plants are easier to find. In spring, a moose's antlers can grow almost 1 inch (2.5 centimeters) each day. By fall, the antlers are fully grown.

Moose shed their antlers one at a time. The second antler is usually shed within 12 hours of the first.

CHAPTER 3

A Moose's Life

When they aren't sleeping, moose spend almost all of their time looking for food or eating. They tend to be most active in the morning and the evening, around sunrise and sunset. A moose might walk for several miles to reach a spot where there is plenty of food. After eating, the animal rests as it digests its meal.

Each moose occupies an area of land known as a **home range**. A home range can vary in size from roughly 1 square mile (2.6 square kilometers) to 35 square miles (91 sq km). The exact location of a home range can change throughout a moose's life. Moose living in some parts of the world might **migrate** dozens of miles as seasons change, to find home ranges with more food, water, or shelter. Though moose are generally **solitary**, they are not **territorial** of their home range.

Moose lie down in comfortable spots when it is time to rest.

Meeting a Mate

While adult moose live on their own for most of the year, they come together during **mating** season in September and October. During this time, males (or bulls) attempt to attract females (or cows) that they can mate with to produce young. One way bulls do this is by making loud, deep sounds called bellows. Interested cows respond with sounds of their own to let the males know where they are. Bulls also rely on the scent of their urine to attract potential mates. A bull usually tries to mate with as many cows as possible each year, while a cow usually mates only once.

When two bulls want to mate with the same female, they often fight each other to establish dominance. They do this by ramming each other with their antlers. These fights usually end before either moose is permanently injured. However, a bull might receive on average dozens of wounds each year.

Male and female moose show that they want to mate with each other by rubbing their faces and muzzles together.

Keeping Calves Safe

After mating, a cow gives birth the following May or June. Usually a single **calf** is born at a time, though moose sometimes give birth to twins. A newborn calf weighs around 30 pounds (14 kg). At first, it survives by drinking milk from its mother. When it is about three weeks old, it can begin eating plants. By the time it is about five months old, it stops drinking milk completely. A calf stays with its mother until she gives birth again the following spring. Then the young moose finds its own home range and soon begins mating and producing calves of its own.

Life is very dangerous for moose calves during the first few weeks of their lives. Though young moose can walk and run, they are small and relatively weak. They depend on their mothers for protection. Predators kill about half of all moose calves during the first six weeks of the calves' lives. However, those moose that survive this period usually live a long time. On average, moose live for around 15 years in the wild, and some have been known to live as long as 22 years.

Baby moose form close, affectionate bonds with their mothers.

CHAPTER 4

Extended Family

All moose belong to the same species. However, scientists have determined that there are enough differences among various groups to divide them into **subspecies**. North American moose can be divided into four subspecies, based mainly on where they live. The Alaskan moose live in Alaska and nearby parts of Canada. The Shiras moose live in the Rocky Mountains. The eastern moose are found in eastern Canada and the northeastern United States, while the northwestern moose live just to the west of that group. Some experts also group Eurasian moose into separate subspecies. However, there is little agreement as to how these moose should be classified.

There are slight differences in size, fur, and antlers among the subspecies. Scientists believe that these differences are a result of each subspecies changing over time to meet the requirements of its habitat.

A Shiras moose polishes its antlers against a branch in Grand Teton National Park.

Moose or Elk?

In Europe, moose are called elk. But while the species known as elk in North America is a relative of the moose, it is not actually the same animal. Like the moose, the elk is a type of deer. It has large antlers, eats plants, and even lives in many of the same areas where moose are found. However, elk are also found in many other places, including regions that would be far too warm for moose to thrive.

While not quite as huge as moose, elk are still very large, making them the second-largest deer species. Another obvious difference between the two species is that an elk's antlers lack the wide, flat shape that a moose's have. Elk have long, narrow **tines** that come to sharp points. Also, instead of leading the solitary lifestyle of moose, elk form huge **herds** containing dozens or even hundreds of animals.

While elk and moose look a lot alike in many ways,
their antlers have very different shapes.

Different Deer

There are more than 40 species of deer living today. These species all belong to the family Cervidae. They are spread throughout much of the world, with species native to every continent except for Antarctica and Australia. One of the most common species is the white-tailed deer, which is native to North America and parts of South America. This deer is named for the distinctive white underside of its tail, which it displays to warn other deer of danger as it flees from enemies.

Another common species is the caribou, or reindeer. Like the moose, this deer thrives in cold weather. It can be found in places such as Scandinavia, Russia, Canada, and even the Arctic. Unlike other deer species, both male and female caribou grow antlers.

The smallest type of deer is the pudu. This tiny deer can weigh as little as 14 pounds (6.5 kg). A large moose weighs almost 100 times that much!

A pudu is around the same size as a house cat.

CHAPTER 5

Moose and Humans

Moose and humans often have difficulties with each other. Many moose habitats are located in or near places where people live. As a result, these moose often come into contact with people as the moose search for food in their home ranges. This can cause big problems. For example, moose are often hit by cars as they cross roads. This happens around 4,500 times each year in Sweden alone, with thousands more accidents in other countries. Because moose are so large, such collisions can cause extreme damage to vehicles. People riding inside are often seriously injured or even killed.

Because moose eat so much food, they can damage farms. It is not uncommon for them to destroy fields full of crops. Moose also eat trees in areas where people are trying to grow new forests. Such behavior can make it difficult to live alongside moose.

Looking out for moose is an important part of everyday driving safety in some parts of the world.

37

Helping Humans

Though they can be troublesome, moose offer many benefits to people. In some parts of the world, these humongous deer are a major source of meat. Moose meat is especially popular in Sweden and other Scandinavian countries. Some people like to drink moose milk and use it to make other dairy products.

Moose are not usually raised on farms. So to harvest their meat, hunters kill moose in the wild. Moose hunting is very popular in some places. Hunters travel from around the world to visit areas where moose are common. Nonhunters often travel to moose-filled areas just to catch a glimpse of these amazing animals in the wild. Businesses in towns and cities where moose are common can make a lot of money by providing services to such tourists.

FUN FACT! Moose cannot sweat. This means they overheat quickly in warm weather.

To attract moose, hunters use calls that imitate the moose's natural sounds.

Today and Tomorrow

Moose are able to defend themselves against many types of threats. However, that has not stopped their numbers from dropping swiftly in some parts of the world, especially throughout North America. Scientists believe that this problem is a result of **climate change**. Moose are meant to live in cold weather, so temperature increases can stress their bodies. In addition, the changing weather has led to an increase in ticks, worms, and other **parasites**. These creatures can infect and kill a healthy adult moose. In one area, higher temperatures led to an increase in beetles. The beetles destroyed huge areas of forest, leaving moose with little food and little shelter from predators.

Despite the fact that moose are slowly disappearing from certain areas, the species as a whole is not **endangered**. In fact, moose populations are growing larger in some parts of the world. However, this does not mean that we should treat them carelessly. In order to ensure the continued survival of moose and other animals, we must work to **conserve** the environment and fight against climate change. With our respect and attention, these remarkable deer will continue to thrive for a very long time.

Protecting the environment will ensure that moose and other wild animals will have the space, food, and shelter they need to survive.

Words to Know

calf (KAF) — the young of several large species of animals, such as moose, seals, elephants, giraffes, or whales

cells (SELZ) — the smallest units of an animal or a plant

climate change (KLYE-mit CHAYNJ) — global warming and other changes in the weather and weather patterns that are happening because of human activity

conserve (kon-SURV) — to protect an environment and the living things in it

endangered (en-DAYN-jurd) — at risk of becoming extinct, usually because of human activity

family (FAM-uh-lee) — a group of living things that are related to each other

habitats (HAB-uh-tats) — the places where an animal or a plant is usually found

herbivores (HUR-buh-vorz) — animals that only eat plants

herds (HURDZ) — groups of animals that stay together or move together

home range (HOME RAYNJ) — the area of land in which an animal usually confines its daily activities

mating (MAYT-ing) — joining together to produce babies

migrate (MY-grayt) — to move from one area to another

muzzle (MUHZ-uhl) — an animal's nose and mouth

parasites (PAR-uh-sites) — animals or plants that live on or inside of another animal or plant

predators (PREH-duh-turz) — animals that live by hunting other animals for food

prehensile (pree-HEN-sile) — adapted for seizing or grasping especially by wrapping around

solitary (SOL-ih-tehr-ee) — preferring to live alone

species (SPEE-sheez) — one of the groups into which animals and plants of the same genus are divided

subspecies (SUB-spee-sheez) — groups of animals that are part of the same species, but share important differences

territorial (terr-uh-TOR-ee-uhl) — defensive of a certain area

tines (TINEZ) — pointed branches of an antler

Habitat Map

PACIFIC

OCEAN

NORTH

AMERICA

ATLANTIC

SOUTH
AMERICA

Moose Range

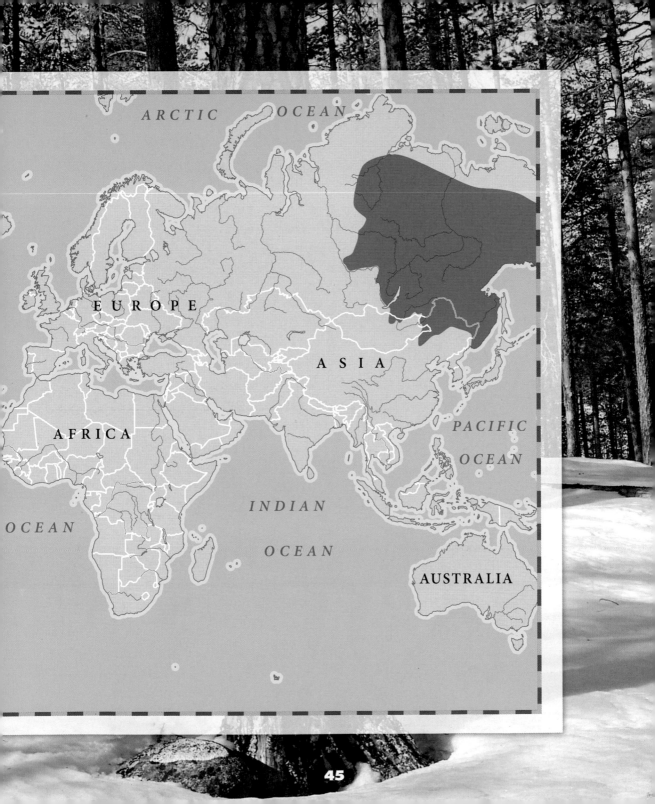

Find Out More

Books

Estigarribia, Diana. *Moose*. New York: Marshall Cavendish Benchmark, 2006.

Riggs, Kate. *Moose*. Mankato, MN: Creative Education, 2012.

Wilsdon, Christina. *Deer*. Pleasantville, NY: Reader's Digest Young Families, 2006.

Visit this Scholastic Web site for more information on moose:
www.factsfornow.scholastic.com
Enter the keyword **Moose**

Index

Page numbers in *italics* indicate a photograph or map.

About the Author

Josh Gregory has written more than 80 books covering a wide range of subjects. He received a BA from the University of Missouri–Columbia. He works as a children's book editor and lives in Chicago, Illinois.